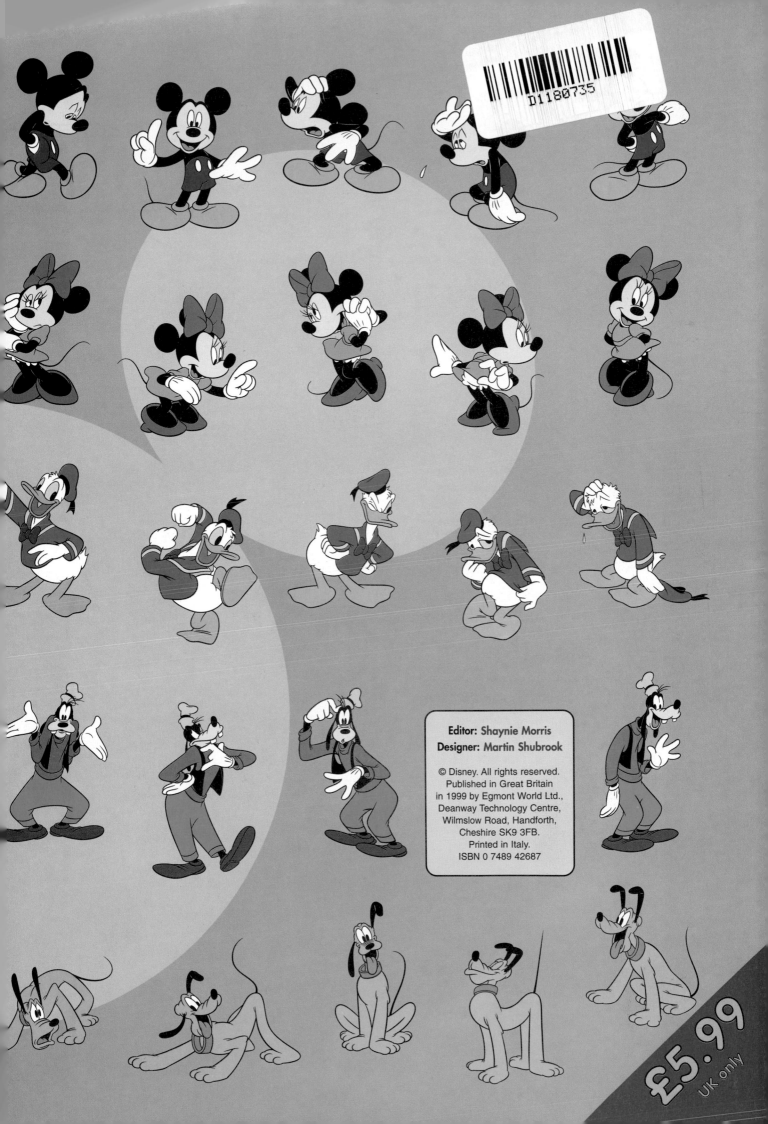

Editor: Shaynie Morris
Designer: Martin Shubrook

© Disney. All rights reserved.
Published in Great Britain
in 1999 by Egmont World Ltd.,
Deanway Technology Centre,
Wilmslow Road, Handforth,
Cheshire SK9 3FB.
Printed in Italy.
ISBN 0 7489 42687

£5.99
UK only

contents

Win a trip to Walt Disney World. Resort
IN FLORIDA

Mickey Mouse and his friends are the most well-known and loved characters in the world. Although Mickey's look has changed since he was first created by Walt Disney in 1928, he will always be the friendly little chap who makes us smile. He entertains us at the cinema, on television, and in books and magazines. Mickey's appeal has lasted for 70 years, and we will continue to love him and his friends well into the new Millennium.

MICKEY

Mickey Mouse is proof that good guys finish first. He's a friendly guy at heart who's always lots of fun and has lots of pals. Mickey is always polite and well-mannered, but has a playful sense of humour. He is a natural-born hero who loves adventure. He often finds himself up against a burly bully or menacing crook, but his quick wits soon get him out of trouble. Mickey is the friend we'd all like to have and the person we'd like to be.

Genuine
Humble
Confident
Adventurous
Cheerful
Clever
A leader
Youthful

First Film:
1928
"Steamboat Willie"

First Feature Film:
1940
"Fantasia"

Mickey phrases:
"That sure is swell."
"Aw, gee..."
"Oh, boy!"

MICKEY MOUSE

A friend in need

Later, at Minnie's house —

I can't **wait** to taste the **blueberry pie** Minnie said she baked today!

Mickey, wait up!

Hector! What are **you** doing here?! And where'd you get that **limousine**?!

Oh, didn't I tell you?! I'm **filthy rich**!

I thought you might need a ride for your date!

Actually, Minnie and I planned a quiet evening at home!

Oh, Mickey! Don't be such a drag!

A drag?! **Me?!**

No dull date tonight! I have ballet tickets and reservations at the Rain Cloud Room for a late supper and dancing!

But... but... what about my **pie**?

I took the liberty of signing your name to the cards, Mickey!

How sweet! I know Mickey **would** have gotten them — if he was only a little more **thoughtful**!

What a **pest**! Why oh why didn't I **wait** and let **Goofy** save his life!

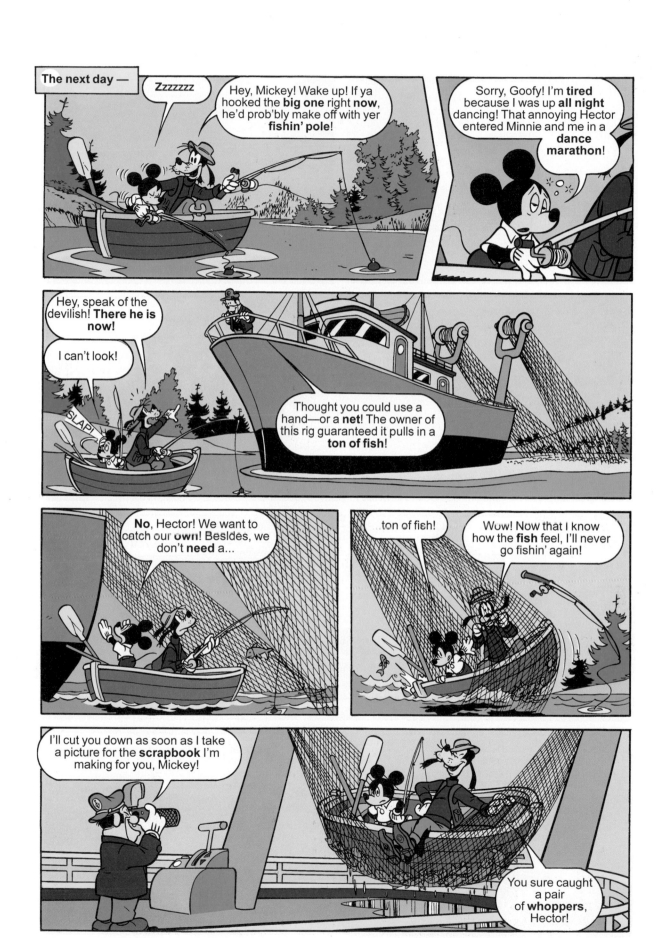

Soon, a desperate plan is hatched —

Gee, it sure is swell that you're **letting me** buy you lunch, Mickey! And that burger joint you suggested looks **great**!

There's Goofy's car, just down the street!

All right, Goofy! We're in position!

There's the signal! Operation **terrify** can now begin!

Mickey said that all I gotta do is try ta run him down!

BZZZZZ

VROOM!

Owwww!

Goofy's doing a great job! It looks like he's **really** out of control!

13

MINNIE MOUSE

Minnie Mouse is always sweet, kind and friendly. Her cheerful, upbeat personality is characterised by her fancy steps and dainty gestures. From the way she walks to the way she talks, Minnie always has a song in her heart.

First Film:
1928
"Steamboat Willie"

Minnie phrases:
"Why, hello!"
"Oh, Mickey..."
"Why, thank you."

Charming
Girlish
Fun-loving
Talented
Sweet
Caring

MINNIE MOUSE

Fool's luck

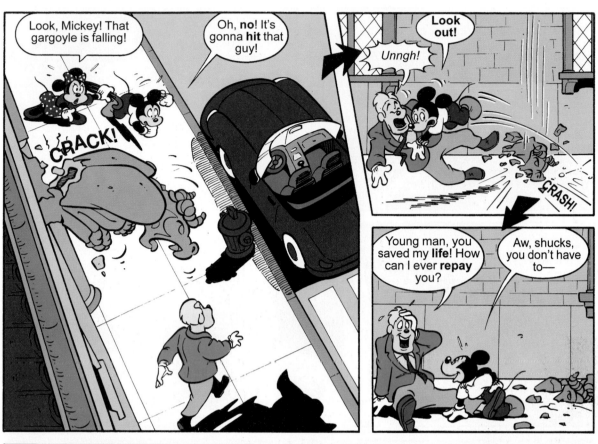

Market mix-up

Mickey and Minnie are buying some fruit from the market. Goofy has noticed that some grapes and apples are mixed in with the other fruits and vegetables. How many apples can you find out of place? How many bunches of grapes?

Answer:
20 apples, 5 bunches of grapes.

25

GOOFY

Goofy is good-natured and has a heart of gold. He is clumsy and hopelessly accident-prone. Goofy tends to do things completely backwards, making simple tasks seem difficult. But despite his approach, Goofy always gets there in the end!

First Film:
**1932
"Mickey's
Revue"**

Goofy phrases:
**"Howdy, Ma'am!"
"Gawrsh!"
"Well, whaddya
know..."**

Simple-minded
Happy-go-lucky
Endearing
Dreamer
Innocent
Clumsy

GOOFY

Loch Mess

Scotland! Land of Celtic mysteries cloaked in swirling fog and —

The **monster!** The monster! I saw the **monster!**

Where? **Where?!** I don't see anything?

Gawrsh!

REWARD FOR PHOTO OF THE LOCH MESS MONSTER!

D 97273

I've got to get a **picture!**

It's just another piece of **driftwood**, Goofy!

I thought for sure **this** time was it!

I'm starting to think we've been **had**, Goofy! We've been here for two days and **this** is all we've got to show for it!

FREE DRIFTWOOD! TAKE ONE!

I'm starting to think that the Loch Mess Monster is just a **fairy-tale!**

Not so, lad!

The monster is no legend! I've seen old **Messy** with these two eyes, and I'll tell you the tale if you'd care to hear it!

Gawrsh, **yes**!

I'll never forget! It was thirty years ago, give or take a day! At sunset a thick **fog** rolled in, covering the whole loch!

"I *should* have headed in for shore, but I just couldn't resist tossing the net in *one* more time!"

"And then, I tell you, it came out of *nowhere*! A *huge* wave that overturned my poor little boat!"

"And then I saw it! A giant *hump* coming at my boat out of the fog! I can only think that my net somehow *disturbed* the monster's slumber!"

Aw, come on! You didn't see anything **except** the hump! It could have been just a **wave**!

A wave, eh? Well, smart boy, take it from me — there are **no waves** in **lochs**!

28

Say, where's your **camera**, Goofy? Have you **given up** monster hunting?

Least till my camera **dries out**! Although I'm startin' to think you were **right** about that monster, Mickey!

ACK!

What's the matter?

The monster! The **monster**! He's right **behind** you!

Where? Where?

Oh, I get it! **Very funny**, Goofy!

No! Really! There he is **again**! The **monster**!

You know, it's not **nearly** as funny the second time around!

Later still —

This is the life, eh, Mickey?

Sure is! Let's just forget about **non-existent** monsters and enjoy our holiday!

I'm going to get some soda at the snack stand! Want anything?

Sure! Get me an orange fizzie!

SPLISH!

Huh? What?

Stop it, Mickey! That **tickles**!

Ha, ha! **Mickey!!!**

Did you call me, Goofy?

Huh? How come you sound like you're so far away, if you're right **here**, Mickey?

SLURP!

ACK! ACK! ACK!

What's with all the **shouting**, Goofy?

SPLASH!

You've got to believe me, Mickey! I **swear** it's true! That monster came right up on the beach and **licked** my face!

Sure, sure, Goofy! But if the monster **is** following you around, why don't you just take a **photo** and win that reward?

That's it! I'll get a picture and **prove** to you that he exists!

Soon —

Now, you're **sure** I've got everythin' I need?

Yes, sir! We dried and cleaned your camera so it's in fine working order!

Still, better take one more roll of film just to be on the **safe** side!

YOUR ONE-STOP, LOCH MESS MONSTER SUPPLY SHOP

Ha! I'll get that monster for **sure**!

One rented boat later —

That sailor said he saw the monster while he was out in the **middle** of the loch, so that's where I'm headin'!

Sure is **foggy** out here! Good thing my camera has a **flash**!

There it is! The **monster**!

That's it! I've **got you** now, Messy! Mickey will **have to** believe me when he sees **these**!

But will he?

Mickey! **Wake up!** This is no time to **sleep**!

Wha—?

Look! Absolute proof positive that Messy **exists**!

It's a **ship**, Goofy! Look — there's the **name** on the bow!

SS BIG BOAT

Horsin' around

Mickey's horse needs some new horseshoes, but Goofy has mixed them up! Can you find the four matching horseshoes?

Answer:
4, 10, 24, 27.

DONALD DUCK

Donald Duck is a friendly and cheerful guy, but when things don't go as planned, he throws outrageous tantrums. He's a practical joker who loves playing tricks on his friends. However, his jokes usually backfire to keep us laughing!

First Film:
1934
"The Wise Little Hen"

Donald phrases:
"Aw, phooey!"
"Nothin' to it!"
"Oh boy, oh boy, oh boy!"

Spirited
Impatient
Hot-headed
Provoking
Outspoken
Assertive

DONALD DUCK

High steppin'

Stay alert, fellas! You never know if we might be spotted by some talent scout from the circus!

Or maybe if there's a flood, we'll be able to wade through the water without getting wet!

This stretch of water might be a little deeper than these stilts can handle!

Hey, kids! Afraid of a little water?

Or the dangerous piranha that might be lurking just under the surface? **Ha-ha-ha-ha-ha-ha!**

What's up with him?

Yeah! Why is he spoiling our fun?

Let's go back home and make some taller stilts! We'll show him who's afraid and who's not!

What's it gonna be?

We can't let him get away with teasing us like this! Any ideas?

He **is** better than us! We'd better be careful what we pick!

How 'bout a race on stilts? Maybe we'll be faster than him!

Okay by me!

Sounds dandy!

Let's have a stilt-race!

Perfect! On **one** condition!

What's the catch?

No catch! I let you pick the contest! You should let me pick the course!

Fair enough!

All right! Tomorrow at dawn, then?!

At dawn it is!

That night — Those kids don't stand a chance against me!

In fact, I have a special surprise planned!

Before long — I want to make sure there are plenty of holes...

...for these termites to feel at home in!

And if that doesn't do the trick, the course goes by some woodpeckers I once had a run-in with!

The woodpeckers won't be able to resist the kids' bug-ridden stilts! But **my** stilts are made of **metal**! Heh-heh-heh!

And so, after dawn — It looks like a heavy storm's brewing!

What's the matter? You afraid of a little rain?

We can't cover ground as fast Uncle Donald any more! Our stilts are too short compared to his tall ones.

The boys were right! It's a flash flood! If they're hurt, it'll all be my fault!

C'mon! Get a move on! There's a giant flash flood!

We can't move very fast!

Grab hold of my stilts! I'll drag you to safety!

Moments later —

You saved us! Hooray!

That's right, boys! But save your thanks until I finish winning this race!

ZZT

Later —

We declared the race a draw!

But we saved you something as a souvenir!

Uncle Donald! You're finally awake!

Gulp!

46

Dashing Donald

Donald has taken quite a few photos of himself, but only one is his favourite!
Read the clues and see if you can figure out which one it is.

Clues
1. It has a red frame.
2. It has a pink background.
3. Donald's eyelids are not showing.

Answer: ↄ

PLUTO

Pluto is a friendly and loyal companion to Mickey who is eager to please his master. Although he is a full-grown dog, he has the playful nature of a puppy. Pluto is full of curiosity, which often gets him into trouble and funny situations!

First Film:
1930
"The Chain Gang"

Pluto phrases:
"Bark! Bark!"
"Grrrr..."
whimpering

Affectionate
Protective
Forgiving
Curious
Jealous
Loyal

PLUTO

A mouse's best friend

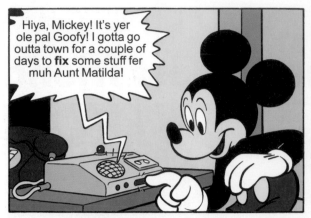

Hiya, Mickey! It's yer ole pal Goofy! I gotta go outta town for a couple of days to **fix** some stuff fer muh Aunt Matilda!

I need you to take care of muh **new puppy** till I get back! Th' little feller's in his kennel on muh kitchen table! Yuh gotta go get him!

I owe ya one! *Click!*

That's **all** we need — a new puppy to take care of! What a **pain**, hey, buddy?!

But what are friends for? Come on! We'd better go **pick up** the little guy!

Shortly, at Goofy's house —

Well, Goofy left a **note**, but where's the puppy?

"Mickey, here's muh **virtual pet**, Sparky! Feed him regular, clean up after him, give him a bath and play with him! Thanks! Yer pal, Goofy!"

Virtual pet?! An electronic gizmo that you have to take care of? Give me a **break**!

It'll never replace the **real** thing, eh, Pluto?

Back at home again —

Take a load off, Sparky! Come on, Pluto! Let's go get a snack!

The next day —

BRRRIIINNG!

Boy, am I **glad** yuh were home, Mickey! How's Sparky?

Hi, Goofy! He's no trouble at all! We're doing swell!

Lissen pal! I entered Sparky in a **virtual pet show** at the Civic Center **this afternoon!** I forgot all about it! Can you take him fer me?!

Well, uh...

Great! I knew I could count on **you**, buddy boy! Bye!

CLICK!

Later that afternoon —

VIRTUAL PET SHOW

I don't believe what **crazy** things I do for my friends! But it's okay — pals like Goofy don't grow on trees!

Very nice! Spike is a **fine** specimen!

You've **got** to be kidding me!

Why, this is a **disgrace!**

Ulp!

This animal is **miserable**! Look at how unhappy he is! When was the last time he was fed?! Played with?!

What sort of monster **are** you?!!

But I... I...

You are a **sorry excuse** for a pet owner! That little creature **depends** on **you**!

I'd be **ashamed** to show my face around **true** pet lovers if I were you!

Gosh, Sparky, I'm **sorry**! I had no **idea** you were so unhappy! I'll do better! I **promise**!

BEEP! BEEP! BEEP!

Not **now**, Pluto! I've got to feed **Sparky**!

SCRITCH! SCRITCH!

Just a **minute**, Pluto! I'm giving Sparky his bath!

BEEP! BEEP! BEEP!

Later that night —

Well, Sparky is all clean and sound asleep! No thanks to **you**, Pluto!

Uh... Pluto? **Pluto?** Hm... he must still be outside!

Pluto! Here, boy! **Pluuuto!** Now **where** can that dog be?!

Not here, either, and it's starting to rain pretty **hard**! The poor mutt is gonna get **soaked**!

PLUTO

That storm is really getting **violent**! I better go look for him!

I **am** a sorry excuse for a pet owner! How could I have left my **best pal** out on a night like **this**?

And it's **my** fault he's gone! I never shoulda **yelled** like I did!

Pluuuuto! Where are you, Pluto?!

Pluto! Oh, Pluto! Thank goodness you're **safe**! I'm so **sorry** I ignored you!

But do you think I would have jumped into a freezing river for that **Sparky**? No way!

He could never replace **you**! You're my very **best** friend! What would I ever do without you?!

Awww, Pluto!

SLURRRP!

And so, the next day —

Well, boy! Time to say goodbye to Sparky! He goes **home** today!

Oh, Sparky-Warky! Daddy **missed** his little snookums! Did Daddy's wittle puppy miss **him**?

Oh, **brother**!

?!?

How could anyone possibly think that some dumb beeping **gadget** could ever replace a real **best friend**?

Arf!

Sort out the shed

Donald has cleared out his garden shed
and there are six things that don't belong in there.
Can you find all six?

Answer:
b, d, k, l, n and p.

Come see Disney's Millennium Celebrations

Win! Win!

at Walt Disney World Resort
IN FLORIDA

Win a fantastic holiday to Walt Disney World® Resort in Florida!

There is an amazing party to celebrate the Millennium, starting on 1st October 1999 for 15 months at EPCOT®. Enter this competition to make sure you're in with a chance of joining in with all the fun!

You'll get to meet all your favourite Disney characters and there will be fantastic shows with lasers, fireworks, special effects and much, much more.

As well as **EPCOT®** you'll be able to visit Walt Disney World's other Theme Parks: **The Magic Kingdom®** Park, **Disney-MGM Studios, Disney's Animal Kingdom®** Theme Park and Disney's three wonderful **water parks**. It's a Disney dream come true!

The Prize:

7 nights accommodation at a Walt Disney World® Resort Hotel for a family of 4 (one room for the winning family) and free entry to all 4 Walt Disney World® Theme Parks and 3 water parks. Prize includes return economy flights from Manchester or Gatwick to Orlando International or Sanford Airport. Meals are not included.

Send your answer, along with your name and address to:

Egmont World Ltd,
Deanway Technology Centre,
Wilmslow Road,
Handforth,
Cheshire SK9 3FB.

How to enter:

Unscramble these letters to spell out a very famous Disney character: KIMCEY

The closing date for entries is the 14th January 2000.